Wil

by Iain Gray

Lang Syne

PUBLISHING

WRITING *to* REMEMBER

LangSyne

PUBLISHING

WRITING *to* REMEMBER

79 Main Street, Newtongrange,
Midlothian EH22 4NA
Tel: 0131 344 0414   Fax: 0845 075 6085
E-mail: info@lang-syne.co.uk
www.langsyneshop.co.uk

Design by Dorothy Meikle
Printed by Printwell Ltd
© Lang Syne Publishers Ltd 2019

ISBN 978-1-85217-675-4

Williams

MOTTO:
True to the kingdom of God
(or)
True to the land.

CREST:
The hunting hound known as a Talbot.

NAME variations include:
William
Williman
Willimon
Wilcox

Chapter one:

Origins of Welsh surnames

by Iain Gray

If you don't know where you came from, you won't know where you're going is a frequently quoted observation and one that has a particular resonance today when there has been a marked upsurge in interest in genealogy, with increasing numbers of people curious to trace their family roots.

Main sources for genealogical research include census returns and official records of births, marriages and deaths – and the key to unlocking the detail they contain is obviously a family surname, one that has been 'inherited' and passed from generation to generation.

No matter our station in life, we all have a surname – but it was not until about the middle of the fourteenth century that the practice of being identified by a particular, or 'fixed', surname became commonly established throughout the British Isles.

Previous to this, it was normal for a person to be identified through the use of only a forename.

Wales, however, known in the Welsh language as *Cymru*, is uniquely different – with the use of what are known as patronymic names continuing well into the fifteenth century and, in remote rural areas, up until the early nineteenth century.

Patronymic names are ones where a son takes his father's forename, or Christian name, as his surname.

Examples of patronymic names throughout the British Isles include 'Johnson', indicating 'son of John', while specifically in Scotland 'son of' was denoted by the prefix Mc or Mac – with 'MacDonald', for example, meaning 'son of Donald.'

Early Welsh law, known as *Cyfraith Hywel*, *The Law of Hywel*, introduced by Hywel the Good, who ruled from Prestatyn to Pembroke between 915 AD and 950 AD, stipulated that a person's name should indicate their ancestry – the name in effect being a type of 'family tree.'

This required the prefixes *ap* or *ab* – derived from *mab*, meaning 'son of' being placed before the person's baptismal name.

In the case of females, the suffixes *verch* or *ferch*, sometimes shortened to *vch* or *vz* would be attached to their Christian name to indicate 'daughter of.'

In some cases, rather than being known for

example as *Llewellyn ap Thomas – Llewellyn son of Thomas* – Llewellyn's name would incorporate an 'ancestral tree' going back much earlier than his father.

One source gives the example of *Llewellyn ap Thomas ap Dafydd ap Evan ap Owen ap John* – meaning *Llewellyn son of Thomas son of Dafydd son of Evan son of Owen son of John.*

This leads to great confusion, to say the least, when trying to trace a person's ancestry back to a particular family – with many people having the forenames, for example, of Llewellyn, Thomas, Owen or John.

The first Act of Union between Wales and England that took place in 1536 during the reign of Henry VIII required that all Welsh names be registered in an Anglicised form – with *Hywel*, for example, becoming Howell, or Powell, and *Gruffydd* becoming Griffiths.

An early historical example of this concerns William ap John Thomas, standard bearer to Henry VIII, who became William Jones.

In many cases – as in Davies and Williams – an s was simply added to the original patronymic name, while in other cases the prefix *ap* or *ab* was contracted to *p* or *b* to prefix the name – as in *ab Evan* to form Bevan and *ap Richard* to form Pritchard.

Other original Welsh surnames – such as Morgan, originally *Morcant* – derive from ancient Celtic sources, while others stem from a person's physical characteristics – as in *Gwyn* or *Wynne* a nickname for someone with fair hair, *Gough* or *Gooch* denoting someone with red hair or a ruddy complexion, *Gethin* indicating swarthy or ugly and *Lloyd* someone with brown or grey hair.

With many popular surnames found today in Wales being based on popular Christian names such as John, this means that what is known as the 'stock' or 'pool' of names is comparatively small compared to that of common surnames found in England, Scotland and Ireland.

This explains why, in a typical Welsh village or town with many bearers of a particular name not necessarily being related, they were differentiated by being known, for example, as 'Jones the butcher', 'Jones the teacher' and 'Jones the grocer.'

Another common practice, dating from about the nineteenth century, was to differentiate among families of the same name by prefixing it with the mother's surname or hyphenating the name.

The history of the origins and development of Welsh surnames is inextricably bound up with the nation's frequently turbulent history and its rich culture.

Speaking a Celtic language known as Brythonic, which would gradually evolve into Welsh, the natives were subjected to Roman invasion in 48 AD, and in the following centuries to invasion by the Anglo-Saxons, Vikings and Normans.

Under England's ruthless and ambitious Edward I, the nation was fortified with castles between 1276 and 1295 to keep the 'rebellious' natives in check – but this did not prevent a series of bloody uprisings against English rule that included, most notably, Owain Glyndŵr's rebellion in 1400.

Politically united with England through the first Act of Union in 1536, becoming part of the Kingdom of Great Britain in 1707 and part of the United Kingdom in 1801, it was in 1999 that *Cynulliad Cenedlaethol Cymru*, the National Assembly for Wales, was officially opened by the Queen.

Welsh language and literature has flourished throughout the nation's long history.

In what is known as the Heroic Age, early Welsh poets include the late sixth century Taliesin and Aneirin, author of *Y Gododdin*.

Discovered in a thirteenth century manuscript but thought to date from anywhere between the seventh and eleventh centuries, it refers to the kingdom of Gododdin that took in south-east Scotland and

Northumberland and was part of what was once the Welsh territory known as *Hen Ogledd*, *The Old North*.

Commemorating Gododdin warriors who were killed in battle against the Angles of Bernicia and Deira at Catraith in about 600 AD, the manuscript – known as *Llyfr Aneirin*, *Book of Aneirin* – is now in the precious care of Cardiff City Library.

Other important early works by Welsh poets include the fourteenth century *Red Book of Hergest*, now held in the Bodleian Library, Oxford, and the *White Book of Rhydderch*, kept in the National Library of Wales, Aberystwyth.

William Morgan's translation of the Bible into Welsh in 1588 is hailed as having played an important role in the advancement of the Welsh language, while in 1885 Dan Isaac Davies founded the first Welsh language society.

It was in 1856 that Evan James and his son James James composed the rousing Welsh national anthem *Hen Wlad Fynhadad – Land of My Fathers*, while in the twentieth century the poet Dylan Thomas gained international fame and acclaim with poems such as *Under Milk Wood*.

The nation's proud cultural heritage is also celebrated through *Eisteddfod Genedlaethol Cymru*, the National Eisteddfod of Wales, the annual festival of music, literature and performance that is held across the nation and which traces its roots back to 1176 when Rhys ap Gruffyd, who ruled the territory of Deheubarth from 1155 to 1197, hosted a magnificent festival of poetry and song at his court in Cardigan.

The 2011 census for Wales unfortunately shows that the number of people able to speak the language has declined from 20.8% of the population of just under 3.1 million in 2001 to 19% – but overall the nation's proud culture, reflected in its surnames, still flourishes.

Many Welsh families proudly boast the heraldic device known as a Coat of Arms, as featured on our front cover.

The central motif of the Coat of Arms would originally have been what was borne on the shield of a warrior to distinguish himself from others on the battlefield.

Not featured on the Coat of Arms, but highlighted on page three, is the family motto and related crest – with the latter frequently different from the central motif.

Echoes of a far distant past can still be found in our surnames and they can be borne with pride in commemoration of our forebears.

Chapter two:

Honours and distinction

A patronymic form of the popular forename 'William', with the final 's' denoting 'son of William' or 'descendant of William', 'Williams' has been present on British shores from medieval times.

Derived from the Old French given name 'Williame' and the Germanic 'Wilhelm', it is of martial roots – with 'will' denoting 'will power' or 'desire to win' in battle, and 'helm' denoting the armoured 'helmet' worn by a warrior.

In Wales, the early heartland of those who would come to bear the Williams name was the ancient kingdom of Brycheiniog – now modern-day Breconshire.

One of the nation's thirteen historic counties, it is also known as Brecknockshire, County of Brecon, County of Brecknock and, in Welsh, as *Sir Frycheiniog* – with 'Sir' denoting 'County'.

The first serious threat to the kingdom's independence came in the sixth century in the form of the Anglo-Saxons – those Germanic tribes who invaded and settled in the south and east of the island of Britain from about the early fifth century.

Composed of the Jutes, from the area of the Jutland Peninsula in modern Denmark, the Saxons from Lower Saxony and the Angles from the Angeln area of Germany, it was the latter who gave the name 'Engla land', or 'Aengla land' – better known as 'England.'

The Anglo-Saxons meanwhile, had usurped the power of the indigenous Britons, who referred to them as 'Saeson' or 'Saxones' – and it is from this that the Welsh term for English people of 'Saeson' derives, the Scottish-Gaelic 'Sasannach' and the Irish-Gaelic 'Sasanach.'

We learn from the *Anglo-Saxon Chronicle* how the religion of the early Anglo-Saxons was one that pre-dated the establishment of Christianity in the British Isles by about 690 A.D.

But, as a form of Germanic paganism with roots in Old Norse religion, it shared much in common with the Druidic 'nature-worshipping' religion of the indigenous Britons such as the Welsh.

The death knell of Anglo-Saxon supremacy was sounded with the Norman Conquest of 1066 when Harold II was defeated at the battle of Hastings, in East Sussex, by a mighty invasion force led by Duke William II of Normandy.

William was declared King of England on

December 25, and the complete subjugation of his Anglo-Saxon subjects followed, with those Normans who had fought on his behalf rewarded with lands – a pattern that would be followed in Wales.

Invading across the Welsh Marches, the borderland between England and Wales, the Normans gradually consolidated their gains – with ancient Welsh kingdoms such as the early Williams heartland of Brycheiniog being taken over by them as 'Lordships'.

Under a succession of Welsh leaders who included Llywelyn ap Gruffudd, known as Llywelyn the Last, resistance proved strong.

But Llwelyn's resistance was brutally crushed in 1283 under England's ruthless and ambitious Edward I, who ordered the building or repair of at least 17 castles and in 1302 proclaimed his son and heir, the future Edward II, as Prince of Wales, a title known in Welsh as *Tywysog Cymru*.

One prominent family of the Williams name hailed from Gwernyfed, in the Brecknockshire parish of Glasbury, with Sir David Williams, born in about 1536, the lawyer and Member of Parliament (MP) for his county who was knighted by James I (James VI of Scotland) and appointed to the King's Bench.

Another prominent family was the Williamses of Cochwillan, and it was one of its sons – who rather

confusingly bore the forename of William – who was the
first to adopt 'Williams' as his surname, the family name
having previously been 'ap Gruffydd'.

His date of birth is not known, but it is known
that he held the important and powerful post of Sheriff
of Caernarvonshire in 1542, 1547 and in 1553, six years
before his death.

High office was also enjoyed by the Williams
family of Tallyn, in the Breconshire parish of Llangasty
Tal-y-llyn, with Sir Thomas Williams, born in 1604,
physician to both Charles II and his successor James II.

Appointed to the lucrative post of Assay-
Master of the Mint as 'payment' for his duties as royal
physician, he died in 1712 – have survived to the
astonishingly ripe old age of 108.

One particularly colourful bearer of the name
was Ann Williams, of the Williams family of Mari,
near Conwy, North Wales, and a branch of the Williams
family of Cochwillan.

Inheriting the property of her brother, Sir
Robert Williams, 7th Baronet, in 1745, she became the
wealthiest heiress in North Wales – but also acquired a
dubious reputation not only because of her extravagant
spending but also because she was reputed to have been
a mistress of Prince William, Duke of Cumberland, and
bore him a son.

She did indeed have a son, who was brought up by her under the name of William Roberts.

Her increasingly spendthrift ways eventually led to the loss of her estates, and she died in poverty in 1770.

Another prominent bearer of the name was Charles Williams, born in 1633 in Caerleon-on-Usk, South Wales.

Having to flee abroad after killing his cousin Morgan of Penrhos in a duel, he settled in modern day Turkey where he amassed a fortune after establishing himself as a merchant.

It was through the influence of a friend, Major John Hanbury of Pontypool, that no action was taken against him for killing his cousin when he returned to British shores, adding to his fortune by trading in stocks and shares and by lending money to the government.

He died in 1720, while in his will he had arranged – as a generous token of thanks to the Hanbury family – for his godson Robert Hanbury, Major Hanbury's son – to inherit £70,000 when he reached the age of majority.

There was only one condition that the unmarried and childless Williams stipulated – that Charles should adopt 'Williams' as his surname.

This was duly done and Charles Hanbury

Williams went on to earn fame as a poet, satirical writer and diplomat and being knighted in recognition.

Sources state that towards the end of his life his 'mind became unbalanced' and, probably by his own hand, he died in 1759 and was buried in Westminster Abbey.

Born in the hamlet of Gwynfe, Carmarthenshire in 1840, John Williams, more formally known as Sir John Williams, 1st Baronet, was not only a physician to Queen Victoria but also a principal founder of the National Library of Wales, in Aberystwyth.

The son of a Welsh Congregational minister, he was raised to his baronetcy by a grateful Queen Victoria in 1894, while he donated his vast collection of manuscripts, books and prints on Celtic matters as the library's 'foundation collection.'

In addition to his royal duties and practice as an obstetric surgeon in London, he was also the driving force behind a major campaign in his native Wales to combat tuberculosis.

He died in 1926, while a book published in 2005, *Uncle Jack*, makes the bizarre claim that he had in fact been the elusive Jack the Ripper, responsible for the gruesome slaying of five women in the Whitechapel area of London in 1888.

Written by one of his alleged descendants,

Tony (Michael Anthony) Williams and co-authored by Humphrey Price, the book claims that all the victims were known to the surgeon and that he killed and mutilated them in a horrific attempt to research the causes of infertility.

Chapter three:

Fame and infamy

Combining politics with the great Welsh literary tradition, Gornowy Williams, better known as Waldo Williams, was the poet, pacifist and Welsh nationalist born in 1904 in Haverfordwest, Pembrokeshire.

The son of a primary school teacher, he followed in his father's footsteps, teaching at schools in his native Wales and also in England.

As a pacifist he refused to pay his income tax during the Korean War of 1950 to 1953, continuing this protest right up until the end of compulsory military conscription in 1963 and being sentenced to imprisonment for his defiant stance.

As a fervent Welsh nationalist, he stood as the Plaid Cymru candidate for Pembrokeshire in the general election of 1959, but failed to be elected.

He died in 1971, noted for Welsh-language poems that include his 1941 *Y tangnefedd wyr – The Peacemakers* and his 1956 *Mewn dau gae – In two fields*.

Also a leading Welsh nationalist, writer and school teacher, David John Williams, better known as

D.J. Williams, was born in 1885 in Rhydcymerau, Carmarthenshire.

A teacher for a time at a school in Fishguard, Pembrokeshire and one of the founders in 1925 of Plaid Cymru, he spent nine months in prison for his part in the 'symbolic' burning of an army bomb-training centre in Penyberth, Northwest Wales.

Renowned as a gifted short story writer and the author of two volumes of autobiography, he died in 1970.

A number of bearers of the Williams name have held high political office.

A Welsh Labour Party politician and barrister, Gareth Wyn Williams, more formally known as Baron Williams of Mostyn, was born in 1941 near Prestatyn, North Wales. Educated at Queen's College, Cambridge, he became a Queen's Counsel, Deputy High Court judge and chairman of the Bar Council.

Created a life peer in 1992 as Baron Williams of Mostyn in the County of Oxfordshire, he served as Opposition spokesman in the House of Lords on legal affairs, while following Labour's election victory in 1997 he became a Home Office minister.

Appointed two years later as Attorney General for England, Wales and Northern Ireland and as Leader of the House of Lords in 2001, he died in 2003.

One of the founding members of the Social

Democratic Party (SDP), Shirley Williams, more formally known as Baroness Williams of Crosby, is the British politician and academic born Shirley Vivian Teresa Brittain Catlin in 1930.

The daughter of the late feminist, pacifist and writer Vera Brittain – whose volume of autobiography *Testament of Youth* was adapted for a film of the name in 2015 – her father was the political scientist and philosopher Sir George Catlin.

Following an education in both Britain and the United States and the holder of a degree in philosophy, politics and economics, she embarked on a career in journalism and worked for a time with the *Daily Mirror* and then the *Financial Times*.

Appointed general secretary of the socialist think-tank the Fabian Society, her full-time career in politics began in 1964 when she was elected Labour MP for Hitchin, Hertfordshire.

Quickly rising through the political ranks, she held a junior ministerial position while between 1971 and 1973 she served as Shadow Home Secretary.

Appointed Secretary of State for Prices and Consumer Protection in 1974, during the premiership of Harold Wilson, she later served in the posts of Secretary of State for Education and as Paymaster General.

Losing her seat when Labour was defeated by

the Conservatives in the general election of 1979, it was two years later that, along with Roy Jenkins, David Owen and Bill Rodgers – and collectively known as the 'Gang of Four' – she founded the SDP.

Another 28 disaffected Labour MPs, also alarmed by increasing far left-wing influence on the party, defected and joined the new party.

Shortly after its formation, Williams won the seat of Crosby in a by-election, but lost it in the 1983 general election.

Unsuccessfully standing for the SDP in Cambridge in the 1987 general election, she later supported the party's merger with the Liberal Party to form the Liberal Democrats.

Moving to work in the United States in 1988, she served until 2001 as a professor at Harvard University's Kennedy School of Government.

Created a life peer in 1993, positions she has since held include Leader of the Liberal Democrats in the House of Lords and commissioner of the International Commission on Nuclear Non-proliferation and Disarmament.

Married from 1955 to 1974 to the moral philosopher Bernard Williams, her second marriage was to the Harvard professor and historian Richard Neustadt, who died in 2003.

One particularly infamous bearer of the otherwise proud name of Williams is the British 'spree killer' Barry Kenneth Williams, a.k.a. Harry Street, who in the space of just over one hour in October of 1978 shot eight people – killing five of them.

A 34-year-old unmarried foundry worker who lived with his elderly parents at the time in the West Midlands town of West Bromwich, as a member of a gun club he had a valid firearms certificate that allowed him to own a semi-automatic weapon.

What was described as his 'erratic behaviour' led to him being expelled from the club: nicknamed "The Cowboy", his disturbing behaviour had included shooting at dummies dressed in wigs and modifying his bullets to make them more powerful.

He had been involved in a number of disputes with his next door neighbours, the Burkitt family, claiming that the volume of noise from their television and record player disturbed both him and his parents.

On one occasion, shortly before his killing spree began, he is said to have told Mr George Burkitt's 20-year-old son, Philip: "I'm going to exterminate you."

Matters came to a deadly head on the evening of October 26, 1978, as Mr Burkitt and his son were working on a car outside their house.

Apparently annoyed by the noise they were

making, Williams approached them and shot both with a 9mm, Smith and Wesson automatic pistol.

George Burkitt was killed on the spot, while his wounded son ran into the house. Williams followed him and shot him again, killing him, while he also shot and killed Mrs Iris Burkitt, the mother.

The family's 17-year-old daughter was also shot, but survived, while two neighbours, a married couple who had witnessed the shootings beside the car, were also shot but survived.

Fleeing the scene in his car and also armed with a .22 calibre pistol in addition to the automatic pistol, Williams shot at two young boys who were playing football, but fortunately missed them.

While passing through the town of Wednesbury, he shot through the windows of a barber's shop and two houses – with a nine-year-old girl being injured by flying glass. Just after 8pm, after stopping to use a road service station at Stockingford, near Nuneaton, Warwickshire, he shot and killed Michel and Lisa Di Maria, the couple who ran it.

Sleeping rough overnight in woodland he was overcome by police and arrested in the town of Buxton after a high speed car chase ended with his car grinding to a halt after being involved in a collision.

Charged with five counts of murder, with two

counts of attempted murder ordered to lie on file, he pled guilty at Stafford Crown Court in March of 1979 to manslaughter on the grounds of diminished responsibility.

After psychiatrists gave evidence that he suffered from "an active paranoid psychosis", his plea was accepted and an indefinite detention – at the high security Broadmoor Hospital and later Ashworth Hospital – was ordered by the judge.

By 1994, however, he was a free man again after a mental health tribunal determined he was no longer a threat to the public.

Going under the name of 'Harry Street', he moved to Wales, where he married in 1996, moving in 2005 to Hall Green, Birmingham.

In October of 2013, police searched his home after a terrified neighbour complained that Williams had been harassing him – and a revolver, two pistols, homemade bullets and an improvised bomb were found.

Pleading guilty at Birmingham High Court to three charges of possessing prohibited firearms, making an improvised explosive device and putting a neighbour in fear of violence, he was ordered to be detained indefinitely under terms of the Mental Health Act 1983.

In making the order, the judge declared: "The effect of these orders is that the defendant may never be released."

Chapter four:

On the world stage

The recipient of a star on the Hollywood Walk of Fame, Robin Williams was the American comedian and actor born Robin McLaurin Williams in Chicago in 1951.

The son of a former model and a senior executive for the Ford Motor Company, his maternal great-great grandfather was the Mississippi senator and governor Anselm J. McLaurin.

Beginning his career as a stand-up comedian on the comedy circuits of San Francisco and Los Angeles, he came to wider attention through his role from 1978 to 1982 of Mork in the television comedy series *Mork and Mindy*.

Noted for his improvisational skills, his big screen debut came in the 1980 *Popeye* while other films include the 1982 *The World According to Garp*, the 1987 *Good Morning, Vietnam* and the 1993 *Mrs Doubtfire*, while he won the Academy Award for Best Supporting Actor for his role in the 1997 *Good Will Hunting*.

A much troubled man, having battled with alcohol and drug abuse and severe bouts of depression, he took his own life in 2014.

Born in 1926 in King's Cross, London, **Kenneth Williams** was the English actor and comedian best known for his roles from 1958 to 1978 in the *Carry On* series of films.

First performing on stage as a member of Combined Services Entertainment during the Second World War, he later featured in radio comedy shows that included Tony Hancock's *Hancock's Half-Hour* and Kenneth Horne's *Round the Horne* and *Beyond Our Ken*.

Characterised by his distinctive voice and also a regular contributor to the BBC radio panel games *What's My Line?* and *Just a Minute*, he died from an overdose of barbiturates in 1988.

An inquest into his death recorded an open verdict, because it was unable to determine if the overdose had been through accident or design.

On British shores, **Olivia Williams** is the English actress of stage, television and film born in 1968 in Camden Town, London.

Having worked with the Royal Shakespeare Company and with television credits that include the 2008 *Miss Austin Regrets*, her major screen credits include the 1996 *Emma*, the 1999 *The Sixth Sense* – starring beside Bruce Willis and the 2002 *The Heart of Me,* for which she won the British Independent Film Award for Best Actress.

Other screen credits include the 2010 *The Ghost Writer*, for which she won the National Society of Film Critics Award and, from 2014, *Maps to the Stars*.

Born in Glan-yr-afon, Mostyn, Flintshire, in 1905, George Emlyn Williams, better known as **Emlyn Williams**, was the Welsh actor and dramatist whose writing credits include the 1935 play *Night Must Fall*, adapted for film two years later and the 1938 *The Corn is Green*, also adapted for film.

With acting credits that include the 1938 *The Citadel*, the 1939 *The Stars Look Down* and the 1942 *Hatter's Castle* – all based on novels by A.J. Cronin – and the recipient of a CBE, he died in 1987.

He was the father of the stage, television and film actor **Brook Williams** and the foreign correspondent and author **Alan Williams**.

Born in 1938, Brook Williams, who died in 2005, had screen credits that include the 1968 *Where Eagles Dare* and, from 1980, *The Sea Wolves*.

His brother Alan, born in 1935, worked for a time as a foreign correspondent for the *Daily Express*.

Compiler along with his then wife Maggie Noach of *The Dictionary of Disgusting Facts*, his other writing credits include the novels *Long Run South*, *The Pink Jungle* and *The Tale of the Lazy Dog*.

On British television screens, David Edward

Williams is the comedian, actor, television presenter and author better known as **David Walliams**.

Born in 1971 in Merton, London, he adopted the surname 'Walliams' when he joined the actors' union Equity because there already was another 'David Williams' on its books.

Best known for his collaboration with fellow actor and comedian Matt Lucas on sketch shows and sitcoms that include *Little Britain* and *Come Fly with Me*, as an author his 2012 book *Ratburger* was selected as Children's Book of the Year by the National Book Awards.

Active in raising substantial sums of money for the Sport Relief charity through arduous feats that have included swimming the English Channel, the length of the River Thames and, along with former rower James Cracknell the 12 mile (19km) Strait of Gibraltar from Spain to Morocco, he won the Landmark Achievement Award at the 2012 National Television Awards.

Also the recipient of an MBE, he has been a judge on the *Britain's Got Talent* television show since 2012.

Behind the camera lens, **Richard Williams**, born in 1933, is the Canadian-British animator best known for his work as animation director on the 1988 *Who Framed Roger Rabbit*.

Author of the 2002 book *The Animator's Survival Kit*, he is the father of the animator and cartoonist **Alex Williams**.

Born in London in 1967, his animation credits include the 1994 *The Lion King*, the 2009 *Harry Potter and the Half-Blood Prince* and, from 2010, *The Chronicles of Narnia: The Voyage of the Dawn Treader*.

Author of a number of plays that were adapted for screen, Thomas Lanier Williams was the great American playwright and author better known as **Tennessee Williams**.

Born in 1911 in Columbus, Mississippi and of Welsh, English and Huguenot descent, his 1955 *Cat on a Hot Tin Roof* and *A Streetcar Named Desire* – which starred Marlon Brando – *The Night of the Iguana* and *Sweet Bird of Youth* are among the plays adapted for film.

The winner of two Pulitzer Prizes he died in 1983, while he was honoured eleven years later in the form of a stamp issued by the U.S. Postal Service as part of its literary arts series.

Bearers of the Williams name have also excelled in the highly competitive world of sport – and no less so than on the tennis court.

Born in 1980, **Venus Williams** and her sister **Serena Williams**, born in 1981, are the American professional players who have both been ranked No.1 in women's singles tennis.

The winner to date of 22 overall Grand Slam titles, including five Wimbledon singles titles, Venus also won Olympic gold medals in 2000 in both singles and doubles.

Serena, winner to date of 18 Grand Slam singles titles and 13 Grand Slam doubles titles with Venus, has won four Olympic gold medals – one in singles and three in doubles.

From the tennis court to the rugby pitch, **Shane Williams** is, at the time of writing, the record try scorer for Wales.

Born in 1977 in Morriston, Swansea and growing up in Glanaman in the Amman Valley and having played club rugby for the Ospreys, he is the most capped Welsh winger.

Retired from international rugby since 2012 and the recipient of an MBE for his services to the game, he has since worked as a radio and television pundit.

From sport to music, Robert Peter Williams is the English singer and songwriter better known as **Robbie Williams**.

Born in 1974 in Stoke-on-Trent, he has enjoyed great success with the band Take That, while as an equally successful solo artist his internationally best-selling singles – some co-written with Guy Chambers – include *Angels*, *Millennium* and *Rock D.J.*

An inductee of the UK Music Hall of Fame after being voted Greatest Artist of the 1990s, he was also the recipient in 2010 of a BRIT Award for Outstanding Contribution to British Music.

On American shores, Hiram King Williams, Sr., was the singer and songwriter better known as **Hank Williams**.

Born in 1923 in Butler, Alabama, his impressive list of self-penned hits – some of which have also been recorded by other artists – include *I'm So Lonesome I Could Cry*, *Hey, Good Lookin'*, *Your Cheatin' Heart*, *Take These Chains from My Heart*, *Long Gone Lonesome Blues* and *Jambalaya (On the Bayou)*.

He died aged only 30, and became the posthumous recipient of a host of honours and awards that include a star on the Hollywood Walk of Fame and induction into both the Country Music Hall of Fame and the Rock and Roll Hall of Fame.

Born in 1927 in Wall Lake, Iowa, Howard Andrew Williams was the American popular music singer better known as **Andy Williams**.

Host from 1962 to 1971 of television's *The Andy Williams Show*, he died in 2012 after having enjoyed success with best-selling albums that include

Moon River, *Days of Wine and Roses*, *Dear Heart* and *Love Story*.

In a much different musical genre, **Ralph Vaughan Williams**, born in 1872 in Down Ampney, Gloucestershire was the acclaimed English composer of choral music, chamber, symphonies, and opera and film scores.

The son of an Anglican Church vicar and a descendant of both Charles Darwin and the potter Josiah Wedgewood, he was aged six when he began to learn to play the piano and, two years later, the violin.

Studying at the Royal College of Music, he went on to compose symphonies that include *Sinfonia Antarctica*, based on his score for the 1948 film *Scott of the Antarctic*.

Also president for a time of the English Folk Dance and Song Society, he died in 1958, while the society's Vaughan Williams Memorial is named in his honour.